NOT TODAY SATAN

Fight the Good Fight of Faith and Win

Dr. Leah McCray

Dr. Leah McCray

Copyright © 2017
Anointed Words Publishing Company
800-496-4153
awpubco@gmail.com
2344 Shawnee Rd., #109
Lima, Ohio
All rights reserved
ISBN: 978-0-9977397-4-9

INTRODUCTION	5
METAMORPHOSIS	7
I'M GOING TO MAKE MYSELF BE SUPERNATURAL	11
MIND RENEWAL	13
THE ENEMY'S DEVICES	16
SIN CONSCIOUSNESS	16
DOUBT & UNBELIEF	19
FEAR	22
A VICTORY MINDSET	24
HE HAS CHOSEN YOU AND SET YOU APART	24
YOU ARE ANOINTED AND APPOINTED	27
YOU HAVE BEEN COMMISSIONED	28
YOU HAVE AN ENEMY, SO BE ONE IN RETURN	31
BUT WHAT DOES GOD SAY ABOUT SATAN AND HIS DEMONS?	32
YOUR SPIRITUAL WEAPONS	34
REPENTANCE	34
FAITH & OBEDIENCE	35
THE WORD OF GOD	36
PRAISE & WORSHIP	38
THE REST OF YOUR ARMOR	40

YOU ARE WELL ABLE TO OVERCOME	**42**

SALVATION CONFESSION:	**44**

POWER ACTION ITEM:	**46**

THANK YOU!	**49**

INTRODUCTION

One day as I was gazing at a stack of bills, thinking on all my visions and dreams that seemed to be drifting out of reach like a cumulus cloud, I lowered my head on the table and closed my eyes.

I've had it. That's it. I'm done.

I knew that I wasn't supposed to be living my life the way that I was living; afraid of this, worried about that and anxious about everything else. And why is there so much lack in my life? I work hard. I don't steal. I don't cheat. What is the problem here? Why aren't I seeing things happen for me? Why do I long for things that never seem to come my way? Why?

So, I sat, waiting for some kind of answer. As I began to suffocate on the silence, I got up and turned off the light and headed for my bedroom. As I got ready to fall face down into my bed, I heard my voice, prompted by the Holy Spirit, begin to rise up inside of me from the pit of my stomach, gaining treble and bass as it reached the deep crevices of my heart and I declared;

"Not today, Satan. Not today!"

METAMORPHOSIS

"And be not conformed to this world: but be ye transformed by the renewing of your mind, that ye may prove what is that good, and acceptable, and perfect, will of God.." – Romans 12:2 KJV.

And so it began. That was the day that I decided to take a stand against the enemy. No more living on pins and needles, wondering what storm is going to hit next, consumed by thoughts of how to avoid the traps, ditches and covered holes that the enemy had hidden across the battlefield that was my life. I decided to take a stand against it. No more. I was determined to live an abundant life, one without fear and without dread. I would stand on the Word of God and heed His command to be strong and courageous.

But how would I do this? Where would I start? I was already saved. I had received Jesus as my Lord and Savior many years ago as a young girl, but what I had learned as an adult; full of mishaps, mistakes, and regret, was that receiving Him *and* allowing Him to live through me were two entirely different things.

Receiving Jesus *and* allowing Him to live through me are two entirely different things

---

Allow me to explain; I am assuming that you have accepted Jesus into your life and that you are saved. Therefore, when you die, you know that heaven is your home. If that is not the case, please go to the last chapter in this book and let me introduce you to Jesus and the wonderful promise that He has for you. After you've done that, come back here and we'll finish up.

But to my saved readers, the reason that Jesus talked so much about the kingdom is because He was teaching us how to live as kingdom citizens, joint-heirs with Him, which we are after salvation.

To Jesus, salvation was the floor. Albeit, a beautiful, necessary, amazing, must-have floor, but still the floor.

What made Him tingle with delight was the thought of us walking in the faith, power and authority that receiving Him, His word and the Holy Spirit would bring. This is what pleases Him; this is what brings glory to His name.

Think about it. Do you remember when Jesus told the disciples to get into the boat because they were going to the other side? During that journey, He fell asleep and a fierce storm arose and they were very afraid.

They were so scared that they woke Jesus up. They were thoroughly amazed that He could sleep through such a storm and they were hoping against all hope that He could do something about it. Jesus, probably annoyed at the intrusion on His naptime but most certainly irritated by their state of unbelief, asked them why they were so fearful and why they had such little faith. Not even bothering to wait for an answer, He spoke to the storm and commanded it to be still as He declared peace in the circumstances. The storm obeyed Him.

Amazed, the disciples inquired amongst themselves as to what kind of man is this that He can command the winds and the waves. They were completely outdone. But, so was Jesus, although for a very different reason.

They were rattled because they didn't know that Jesus could talk to storms and command them to obey, and Jesus' irritation was because He knew that they hadn't come to the understanding that they could.

I'm going to make myself be supernatural

Well, I was not going to sit in this boat, being swept away by seas of circumstance. I was determined to be supernatural. I would make myself be supernatural.

But what is that? What is super about being natural? About operating in this flesh? So to "super it up" would mean to just be natural on steroids. So just more of what I already am, more of that fleshy stuff? No thank you!

What I was willing to believe, accept & receive, was what I had become & what was being manifested in my life every day

---

The desire is to be spiritual. And, with that, there's no need to be *super-spiritual*, for being in the spirit is being led and directed by God, so there are no levels. There is one Spirit of God and my desire is to flow in Him.

So, if you're in the spirit, you're in the place of blessing. It is the enemy who tells us to say more than yes or no. He convinces us to embellish, elaborate and dress up things that should simply be this or that. So, no, I don't need to walk in the supernatural, just in the Spirit of the Most High God!

So, when I began to look at all that was not right in my life; the lack, the shame, the lost hope, the depression, the oppression. Whatever it was, I realized that I was here because I allowed myself to be here.

I was being natural while trying to be super at it; and it all began in my mind. What I was willing to believe, accept and receive was what I had become and what manifested in my life every day. *I needed a transformation, a kingdom metamorphosis, and you can only get that by getting the word of God.*

Mind Renewal

So, the *Word* said that we are to be transformed by the renewing of our mind. So what does the word say about our minds? What does it say about how we should be thinking about ourselves and our lives? And once we have that answer, how do we apply it?

You are not the same. "for you have been born again [that is, reborn from above--spiritually transformed, renewed, and set apart for His purpose] not of seed which is perishable but [from that which is] imperishable and immortal, that is, through the living and everlasting word of God." 1 Peter 1:23 AMP

It all starts here. Every other truth and promise are built upon and accessed through this powerful life-giving truth. **You have been re-born**. What does that mean? What mind-renewing, life transforming nugget lays within this statement? Ready? Here we go!

You have become new. Try and recall every negative thing that you've ever thought about yourself and every negative thing that anyone has ever said about you, and understand that that person has died. You are a new creation.

The you before Jesus was a slave to sin, unable to get free of habits and emotions that were rooted in selfishness, greed, fear, jealousy or hatred. The old you really didn't even see anything wrong with taking care of self before anything or anyone else, at any cost.

You are not your past

But think about what began to happen on the inside of you when you thought, spoke or behaved as you may have in the past, before you accepted Christ. Why is there a pause that happens now before you do or say something hurtful? Why the remorse? Why the conviction?

Because, my friend, you have been reborn. You are not the same person, even if you sometimes act like it. You must wrap your mind around this truth and accept it. Once you do, it will be much easier for you to act in accordance with who you are now and who you are becoming. Oh yes, you are righteous right now, in spite of your mistakes you are becoming a "son of God."

So, not only have you been reborn into this newness of life, which is actually a throwback to what you were from the beginning; made to live and operate in the earth as God does in heaven, but, you have also been reborn into an eternal life of oneness with Him.

So, the first step to kicking Satan out of your affairs and transforming your life by the renewing of your mind is to fully embrace, acknowledge and understand that you have been born (received your place) into the Kingdom of God. Think on this a while and don't move off it until you really get the enormity of it all.

THE ENEMY'S DEVICES

Sin Consciousness

You are forgiven on the account of Jesus' name and His blood that was shed for you. That's it, that's all. There is nothing that you could ever do to pay your debt.

1 John 2:12 states, "I am writing to you, little children (believers, dear ones), because your sins have been forgiven for His name's sake [you have been pardoned and released from spiritual debt through His name because you have confessed His name, believing in Him as Savior]."

So, I repeat, you are FORGIVEN! You need to really grab a hold of this truth because one of the most effective weapons that the enemy uses against the people of God is a gnawing feeling of unworthiness. That we've gone too far; done way too much.

Even after we have received salvation, many of us will stop right there, breathing a sigh of relief and go no further into Kingdom reality because we believe that we have really just made it in by the skin of our teeth, and that to expect anything more from God is just foolish.

However, the truth is that to even expect salvation from God based on our own merit or ability is a fool's perspective. We were saved because we accepted Jesus as our Lord and Savior and as the propitiation (payment of debt) for our sin.

God forgave us not because we were sad, or hurt, or determined to never do such things again. All these are a right response to sin in our lives, but they do not move God's divine commitment to justice nor relieve us from the due wages of sin, which is death. But what does move God is the blood of Jesus. We have been forgiven, once and forever, as long as we stay under The Blood.

One of the most effective weapons that the enemy uses against the people of God is a gnawing feeling of unworthiness

So the next time the enemy tries to assault your mind with thoughts that God is angry with you or that you are on the "outs" with God, tell him, ***not today*** and simply remind him and yourself that it is the Blood that has purchased your forgiveness and your freedom. The blood of Jesus, all by itself, is more than enough. ***Renew your mind on that!***

Doubt & Unbelief

How destructive is doubt & unbelief? Let's examine two scriptures and see what God has to say about the importance of not being sidelined by this double-barreled shotgun:

First, Mark 11:22-24; "So Jesus answered and said to them, "Have faith in God. For assuredly, I say to you, whoever says to this mountain, 'Be removed and be cast into the sea,' and does not doubt in his heart, but believes that those things he says will be done, he will have whatever he says. Therefore I say to you, whatever things you ask when you pray, believe that you receive them, and you will have them." Mark 11:22-24 NKJV

In this scripture, we can clearly see that doubt and unbelief will cause our declarations and prayers, which are based on and rooted in God's word, to have no power to manifest. Our God is telling us very plainly that to receive from Him when we pray, we must cast doubt and unbelief aside. We must consider it already done.

Now let's look at James 1:5-8; "If any of you lacks wisdom, let him ask of God, who gives to all liberally and without reproach, and it will be given to him. But let him ask in faith, with no doubting, for he who doubts is like a wave of the sea driven and tossed by the wind. For let not that man suppose that he will receive anything from the Lord; he is a double-minded man, unstable in all his ways." James 1:5-8 KJV

Wow! In this word is the revelation that whatever we are seeking from God, we must ask in faith, fully assured that He is not only ABLE to supply the very thing that we are in need of, but that He is also WILLING. We must not waiver in this because if we are "wishy-washy" in our stand on the faithfulness of God, not only can we expect not to receive, but get ready to suffer loss. This is a very real warning to the body of Christ and a clear instruction on how to walk in victory in this Kingdom life.

I also like this verse on being single-minded when it comes to the Word of God; "The light of the body is the eye: if therefore thine eye be single (keep on one thing, no alternative, consider not...), thy whole body shall be full of light. But if thine eye be evil, thy whole body shall be full of darkness. If therefore the light that is in thee be darkness, how great is that darkness!" Matthew 6:22-23 KJV

We must not waiver in this because if we are "wishy-washy" in our stand on the faithfulness of God, not only can we expect not to receive, but get ready to suffer loss

---

Keep your heart, mind, and SPEECH on one thing only; *what does God say about it.* Believe His report. No back-up plan, no alternative outcome, only what God has said. This is how we make our way prosperous and defeat the enemy's tactics.

So, remember, don't let TIME make you DOUBT what God told you WOULD happen. Stand on His word, in faith, no matter what. Give doubt and unbelief no place in your heart.

Fear

"Fearing people is a dangerous trap, but trusting the LORD means safety." Proverbs 29:25 NLT

God tells us in 2 Timothy 1:7, that He "has not given us the spirit of fear, but of power, of love, and of a sound mind." So if fear doesn't come from God, it comes from the enemy.

Our father tells us multiple times in scripture to not be afraid. Why, because fear paralyzes us in our pursuit of our purpose. Fear causes us to fall back, to rationalize, and ***to walk in reason and not in faith***. Fear is faith in what the devil wants to do to us and its seed is unbelief.

The antidote to fear, however, is quite simple; just spend time with Jesus! "Now when they saw the boldness and unfettered eloquence of Peter and John and perceived that they were unlearned and untrained in the schools [common men with no educational advantages], they marveled; and they recognized that they had been with Jesus." Acts 4:13 AMP

The antidote to fear is spending time with Jesus

Simply basking in the power-laden presence of The Lord and spending time in His Word will give you a strength and a boldness that you never knew you were capable of having. In His presence there is peace and in His Word there is life.

A VICTORY MINDSET

He Has Chosen You and Set You Apart

You are a member of a chosen race, a royal priesthood, a holy nation, a People for God's own possession. (1 Peter 2:9,10). "But you are A CHOSEN RACE, A royal PRIESTHOOD, A CONSECRATED NATION, A [special] PEOPLE FOR God's OWN POSSESSION, so that you may proclaim the excellences [the wonderful deeds and virtues and perfections] of Him who called you out of darkness into His marvelous light. Once you were NOT A PEOPLE [at all], but now you are GOD'S PEOPLE; once you had NOT RECEIVED MERCY, but now you have RECEIVED MERCY." 1 Peter 2:9-10 AMP

Now, knowing that you have been born again and that you have been forgiven, who are you? What is your identity at this point?

You have been re-born into a distinct, definitive, devil-defeating dynasty

Often when you accept Jesus and come into the kingdom of God, you feel different and alone. When you make daily decisions to live a life that honors God by conforming your thoughts and your behaviors to be like Christ, It may feel like it's you against the world and, frankly, it is.

Sociologists tell us that we, human beings, need to feel a part of something, need to feel as though we belong. This is why, they say, kids that feel abandoned, unloved and alone join gangs and other unhealthy social groups and situations, just to be a part of something.

Your heavenly Father wants you to know that if every person that you have called family or friend turns against you because of your commitment to serve him, that He will never leave you, nor forsake you. So, although you may feel alone at times, like you are walking this life alone, what is the truth? Let's chew on this mind-renewal nugget; you have been re-born into a distinct, definitive, devil-defeating dynasty.

Not only are you now supernaturally linked up with believers all over the world, but you have angels that surround you and go before you, a mass of witnesses in the heavenlies cheering you on and the Holy Spirit of God living on the inside of you.

So the next time the enemy serves up the lie that you have been deserted in order to lure you into depression while convincing you that the cure for an ailment that you *don't really have* is found in the world; just give him that word; "I am a chosen race, a royal priesthood, God's own possession" and watch him scurry out of the room.

You Are Anointed and Appointed

"As for you, the anointing [the special gift, the preparation] which you received from Him remains [permanently] in you, and you have no need for anyone to teach you. But just as His anointing teaches you [giving you insight through the presence of the Holy Spirit] about all things, and is true and is not a lie, and just as His anointing has taught you, you must remain in Him [being rooted in Him, knit to Him]." 1 John 2:27 AMP

He has gifted you. He has placed in you His anointing that has the ability to supply you with everything that you will ever need. It's all in there because you are in Christ and He is in God.

You Have Been Commissioned

Now that you know who you are and whose you are, that your sins have been forgiven, that you are a new creation born into a family whose personal and intimate Father is almighty God; how can you possibly live up to the hype?

I know that's not a word we would normally associate with believers, but the world does. They say no one can live their lives based on the writings of "that old, obsolete book." Who can obey all those "rules?" Additionally, even if this "Jesus" healed people, forgave sins, freed the bound and raised the dead, that was way back then, in another age and time. Do they really believe that they can do that stuff today?

Wrap your minds around the Word, people of God, not only did Jesus say you can do all of that, but He has commissioned you to do it. Let's unpack this.

First, where in scripture can we point to the fact that Jesus delegated His authority to us? In Mark 6:7-13, Jesus sends the disciples out in groups of two, telling them that He is sending them out with power over unclean (demonic) spirits, to preach repentance, cast out many devils and to heal the sick. Is there any difference between the disciples and you? The word "disciple" as used in the text, simply means "one that is sent by God." Have you been sent? What does the Word say? Ready? Meditate wholeheartedly on this:

You have been empowered and deployed in this world to be like Jesus

---

"But now I am coming to You, and I say these things [while I am still] in the world so that they may experience My joy made full and complete and perfect within them [filling their hearts with My delight]. I have given to them Your word [the message You gave Me]; and the world has hated them because they are not of the world and do not belong to the world, just as I am not of the world and do not belong to it. I do not ask You to take them out of the world, but that You keep them and protect them from the evil one. They are not of the world, just as I am not of the world. Sanctify them in the truth [set them apart for Your purposes, make them holy]; Your word is truth. Just as You **commissioned** and sent Me into the world, I also have **commissioned** and sent them (believers) into the world. For their sake, I sanctify Myself [to do Your will], so that they also may be sanctified [set apart, dedicated, made holy] in [Your] truth. "I do not pray for these alone [it is not for their sake only that I make this request], but also for [all] those who [will ever] believe and trust in Me through their message, that they all may be one; just as You, Father, are in Me and I in You, that they also may be one in Us, so that the world may believe [without any doubt] that You sent Me." John

17:13-21 AMP

So, now there can no longer remain any doubt that you have been empowered and deployed to be as He is in this world. One person who believes Him can change the future and redeem the past. One person who walks in His resurrection power is like a one-man (or woman) wrecking crew – busting up Satan's devices, schemes and attacks everywhere he or she goes. When we truly believe the word of God, there is nothing that can stop us.

You Have an Enemy, So Be One In Return

Don't get it twisted; you are in a fight! An enemy is defined as one who fosters harmful designs against another, an armed foe; an adversary or opponent. 1 Peter 5:8 tell us to "Be sober, be vigilant; because your adversary the devil, as a roaring lion, walketh about, seeking whom he may devour:"

Because he knows who you are and what you possess, this enemy hates you, and he intends to gain and keep a stronghold in your life. Satan, the enemy of your soul, has only one mission concerning you and that is to steal, kill and destroy.

But What Does God Say About Satan and His Demons?

"He canceled the record of the charges against us and took it away by nailing it to the cross. In this way, he disarmed the spiritual rulers and authorities. He shamed them publicly by his victory over them on the cross." Col 2:14-15 NLT

"Blotting out the handwriting of ordinances that was against us, which was contrary to us, and took it out of the way, nailing it to his cross; and having spoiled principalities and powers, he made a shew of them openly, triumphing over them in it." Col 2:14-15 KJV.

So, again, why were we ever in fear? **Jesus disarmed him on the cross!**

YOUR SPIRITUAL WEAPONS

Repentance

We must judge ourselves so that we will not be under judgment. What does this mean? When we sin, we must immediately confess it to our Father, agree wholeheartedly with His Word and ask for forgiveness. When we do this, we take ourselves out of the judgment zone where the enemy can get access to our lives and puts us right back into righteousness under the protection and provision of God.

God's desire is to bless you and to not allow judgment to enter, but he is a just God. He cannot remain where sin is present. It is a separating force. So, judge yourself and close the door on the enemy for good.

Faith & Obedience

The Hebrew word for 'faith' - emunah - is less about KNOWING and more about DOING. 'Emunah' literally means "to take firm action", so to have faith is to *act*. It's like a staircase; you may intellectually know that the stairs go up to the next level, but until you climb the stairs you won't experience the next level. What you do is more important than what you know. Don't just believe in the stairs, climb the stairs. Faith without works is dead. James 2:17.

Faith is like a staircase; you can see it goes up to the next level but until you climb it, you won't experience the next level

---

Faith is being willing to believe God enough to look ridiculous and be maligned like Noah; to go someplace that you have never been and prosper like Abraham; to believe that you can win a seemingly unwinnable fight like David, Joshua and Gideon; to trust God enough to give out of your lack like the widow woman; to face down danger and threats like Esther or to do the impossible like Peter, just to name a few. If you don't take the risk you forfeit the miracle. In obedience the blessing is manifested.

The Word of God

"So then faith comes by hearing and hearing by the word of God." Romans 10:17. Our only offensive weapon is God's word. It is spirit and it is life. It will cut the enemy off at the knees.

In times of trouble and out, the Word of God and speech that aligns itself with it, should be the only confession that comes out of your mouths. This is how you resist the enemy and cause him to flee. Using this weapon causes what the enemy had planned for evil in your life to be rendered useless.

Additionally, you derive wisdom, strength, and power in all areas of your being from declaring and confessing God's Word in faith. It is your most powerful weapon and you must get it into your heart and on your lips.

Your anointed words have the power & force of heaven behind them

---

Praise & Worship

"About midnight Paul and Silas were praying and singing hymns to God, and the prisoners were listening to them, and suddenly there was a great earthquake so that the foundations of the prison were shaken. And immediately all the doors were opened, and everyone's bonds were unfastened. When the jailer woke and saw that the prison doors were open, he drew his sword and was about to kill himself, supposing that the prisoners had escaped. But Paul cried with a loud voice, "Do not harm yourself, for we are all here." And the jailer called for lights and rushed in, and trembling with fear he fell down before Paul and Silas.

Then he brought them out and said, "Sirs, what must I do to be saved?" And they said, "Believe in the Lord Jesus, and you will be saved, you and your household."
And they spoke the word of the Lord to him and to all who were in his house. And he took them the same hour of the night and washed their wounds, and he was baptized at once, he and all his family.

Then he brought them up into his house and set food before them. And he rejoiced along with his entire household that he had believed in God." Acts 16:25-34

Praise is a weapon. When it is used in the midst of attack, it is like you are laughing in the face of the enemy and it instantly demoralizes him and brings glory to God.

God says position yourself for victory by advancing with praise & worship

---

The devil is not omniscient. He thinks that what he brings to you will devour you, but when you keep praising, looking at the promise, not the problem while hiding yourself in Christ, he and his host are resigned to the truth that they cannot stop you from your inheritance.

The fight is fixed. Your victory assured!

The Rest of Your Armor

Take some time to read and re-read Ephesians 6:10-16, getting it deep into your heart. This is your entire armor. If you make sure that you are fitted with everything that is listed here, you will never again walk in defeat. But it is important to get revelation of this Word. Pray and ask God to reveal the application of this Word in your life.

10 A final word: Be strong in the Lord and in his mighty power. 11 Put on all of God's armor so that you will be able to stand firm against all strategies of the devil. 12 For we[ ] are not fighting against flesh-and-blood enemies, but against evil rulers and authorities of the unseen world, against mighty powers in this dark world, and against evil spirits in the heavenly places.

¹³ Therefore, put on every piece of God's armor so you will be able to resist the enemy in the time of evil. Then after the battle you will still be standing firm. ¹⁴ Stand your ground, putting on the belt of truth and the body armor of God's righteousness. ¹⁵ For shoes, put on the peace that comes from the Good News so that you will be fully prepared.[ ] ¹⁶ In addition to all of these, hold up the shield of faith to stop the fiery arrows of the devil.[ ] ¹⁷ Put on salvation as your helmet, and take the sword of the Spirit, which is the word of God.

¹⁸ Pray in the Spirit at all times and on every occasion. Stay alert and be persistent in your prayers for all believers everywhere.[ ]

YOU ARE WELL ABLE TO OVERCOME

With God all things are possible and He is with you at all times. In the light of that truth and the truth that you have been reminded of throughout this book, **take your stuff back!** Go and recover all. Don't let the enemy steal anything from you, kill anything that God has given life to or destroy any good thing in your life. You have victory in Jesus. He has given you the tools to fight the good fight of faith. Use them and rest in the overcoming power of Christ.

In closing, here are ten promises from God that will change your life if you really believe them and receive them, they are:

- **You are forgiven.**
- **God is not angry with you.**
- **You are righteous right now.**
- **You are healed.**
- **God will take care of you.**

- You have been redeemed from the curse of the law
- You have the mind of Christ (wisdom, discernment, revelation).
- You know His voice so you can trust your conscious (unctions).
- You can rest.
- He gave you dominion, power, and authority.

SALVATION CONFESSION:

"Father, God, I know that you are real and I am coming to you acknowledging my need for a Savior.

I believe that Jesus is the Son of God and that He shed His blood for me. I ask that you forgive me for my sins and I believe that Jesus took my punishment on the cross so that I could be reconciled to you and made whole.

I accept Jesus in my life today as my Lord and Savior and I thank you."

Hallelujah!!!

You are now part of the Kingdom of God. If you are not in a bible believing and bible teaching church, please find one so that you can continue to grow in the Lord and live the abundant life that He came to restore to you.

Not Today Satan

Please contact me and let me know of your confession so that I can be praying for you.

God bless you! Love you!

POWER ACTION ITEM:

"It is the glory of God to conceal a thing and the honor of kings to search out a matter" Proverbs 25:2. KJV

If you will take the time to search out every one of the ten promises listed above, not only will that help you to remember them when you need those truths the most, but you will be richly blessed as God honors your efforts to search Him out.

List your Scripture references for the ten promises here:

1._____

2._____

3._____

Not Today Satan

4._____

5._____

6._____

7._____

8._____

9._____

10._____

Excerpt from "100 Day Devotional; 100 Words in 100 Days to a Changed Life & Restored Purpose."

Faith – belief that is not based on proof.

"Faith that does nothing is worth nothing. James 2:20." NCV

Faith is confidence and trust in a person or a claim made, which ultimately rests on the confidence or trust in the person MAKING the claim or promise. But faith doesn't end there. Real faith is only complete when you couple a corresponding action with that confident belief.

Faith is a creative spirit. It creates and gives power to manifest the very things for which you are believing…

Faith harnesses the power of God. Hebrews 11.

THANK YOU!

Dear friend, thank you for taking this journey with me. Your companionship so honors me and I pray that God will continue to bless your life in amazing ways.

Remember above all else that He loves you and He will equip you to meet every challenge that life may bring. Trust in His faithfulness for He will never fail you.

Please feel free to write to me at Leahmccray.com or leave a comment on my Facebook page at L.T. McCray. I would love to hear from you.

Until then, my love and prayers are with you and your family.

In His loving grace,

Minister Leah

Some other books by Dr. Leah McCray:

100 Day Devotional: 100 Words in 100 days to a changed life & renewed purpose.

The Kingdom Wife.

I Declare! You're faith filled words have the power to change things.

(Available on Amazon.com)
Or Visit:
leahmccray.com
FB@drltmccray
or
awpubco.com

www.ingramcontent.com/pod-product-compliance
Lightning Source LLC
Chambersburg PA
CBHW032113040426
42337CB00040B/572